SCULPTOR OF THE NORTH
The Evolution of a Soul

SCULPTOR OF THE NORTH
The Evolution of a Soul

Doug Petersen

ARPress
45 Dan Road Suite 5
Canton MA 02021

Hotline: 1(888) 821-0229
Fax: 1(508) 545-7580

Ordering Information:

Quantity sales. Special discounts are available on quantity purchases by corporations, associations, and others. For details, contact the publisher at the address above.

Printed in the United States of America.

ISBN-13:   Softcover   979-8-89330-872-3
             eBook   979-8-89330-873-0
Library of Congress Control Number: 2024901881

Table Of Contents

Acknowledgements I

Epigraph III

Preface VII

Chapter 1 1

Chapter 2 3

Chapter 3 4

Chapter 4 5

Chapter 5 6

Chapter 6 9

Chapter 7 11

Chapter 8 13

Chapter 9 14

Chapter 10 16

Chapter 11 18

Chapter 12 19

Chapter 13 20

Chapter 14 22

Chapter 15 23

Chapter 16 25

Chapter 17 26

Chapter 18 27

Chapter 19 28

Chapter 20 30

Chapter 21 32

Chapter 22 34

Chapter 23 36

Chapter 24 37

Largest Cement Human Figure in Minnesota 41

Postscrip 45

Acknowledgements

Jim Morrison – My Mentor

Phil and Kathy Potterjoy – My Friends

My Grandparents Ed and Inez my parents Bernice and Ken Jim Mvorrison whose poetry inspired me and Michell Fowler who helped in the editing of this book.

Epigraph

Fealty to Winter

Colder than a witches kiss.

Dedicated to Kit Kat
My best friend for 18 years.

July 10, 2004
July 28, 2021

It is in part why I dedicated this book to the Potterjoys as we have been friends for more than 40 years.

I should have included my faithful and tough best and only friend while living in the remodeled horse barn.

I should have included him in the acknowledgements page. Lemmon his name was.

He was eaten by wolves in the late '80' s.

Lemmon was a blind Great Pyrenees dog that I found out wandering around and howling like he needed help and of course one look at his cataract clouded eyes told me why;

Ole Lem was a tough, shaggy, white long furred dog who was blind yet somehow followed me to work at Bear Head Lake State Park. He once in fact brought a dead rabbit to the horse barn remodeled log cabin.

I would let him out of the warm cabin at night fall when he could cool off at night.

He would usually wind up howling away and I would strap on the .22 calibre pistol and trudge through the brush flash light in hand howling for Lemmno to howl back so I could better pin point his location out in the woods at night.

No wonder animals like bear and deer have a much more highly heightened sense of hearing than humans do.

I would eventually locate Lemmon out in the woods fighting his way through the brush. He was a tough dog who adapted to his new sightless world. Animals do not know the uniqueness of honor. Honesty is uniquely human. Animals teach their human friends patience and tranquility.

Preface

On May 4, 1970, a beautiful and sunny day, the cops bore down on us swinging billy clubs and spraying tear gas snuffing out the clean sunshine and changing the path of my life. It was the bombing of Cambodia by the United State's air force and the ensuing protests across college campuses in America bringing down the curtain and opening up a narrow crack in a largely imaginary door in my mind.

Chapter 1

When old enough to count a bicycle and a baseball glove as part of my possessions, I was used to hanging out in the garage or down in the basement tinkering with all sorts of tools and interesting looking things that I would find down there. Great places to be playing with matches or exploring the creation of a rocket or at least a bomb. When not playing evil genius in his workshop, I was at some field or pasture, within range of my bicycle, playing baseball. Despite my best effort, I was not destined to be a major-league baseball idol. My home was in Richfield, Minnesota, a southern suburb of Minneapolis. The house, largely built by my father, was a small 2-bedroom bungalow situated on a lot purchased from the next door farmstead. At the age of 12, while in the 6th grade, Chloriss Hoksch, my teacher, gave all of us kids some great advise. Grow a thick skin, you will need it.

I led a pretty normal and peaceful childhood that had a few highlights. I graduated from playing baseball and the piano to making bombs and then onward to drag racing in my rebellious teenaged years. My police record was pretty thin. Just an occasional speeding ticket and an incident where I supposedly started a riot. Of some sort, I could not possibly have done that since I was passed out drunk in Paul's car in the parking lot of Country Kitchen. Lucky--no jail and no declaration of being a public enemy and given the heave-ho out of town. I did graduate in 1969 though, and soon after was on my own. It was the beginning of an adventure. I opened my eyes to what had been not in my sight. Now that I look back, it was completely impossible for me to have imagined the fulness and complexity of the ride I was about to take. When I was 14, I saved my nickels and dimes to buy a 1953 Cushman Eagle. I of course, did not yet have a driver's license. But that didn't stop me. I rode my prized iron horse all over town even to confirmation class which I got the boot from. Poor Pastor Sveum, my Lutheran spiritual guide. Eventually, he's tired of my disruptions and booted me. Everything was hilarious to me and with so many laughing at my antics he had no choice.

Chapter 2

Before that I rode my bicycle everywhere and especially to Metropolitan Stadium home of the Minneapolis Millers a minor league baseball team and later the Minnesota Twins and Vikings'.

It was 1965 a historic year for Minneapolis in several ways.

The Beatles performed at Metropolitan Stadium for their first and only appearance in Minnesota on August 25th. Ambulances were parked outside just in case they were needed to cart off hysterically and fainting teenaged girls.

I was used to being in the stadium as I had VIP access by way of a crescent wrench. It was my pass key. Like a cat burglar, I undid the bolts holding the bolts on the bars of the turnstiles. I carefully chose which one to open up so I could squeeze through. The one beyond the left field fence which was about as far away from curious people who could see what I was up to as you could get.

Chapter 3

That was my way into the stadium for baseball games for 5 years or so. Metropolitan Stadium was a triple decker with bleachers in the outfield. It held about 40,000 people and was open to the skies.

I made my way through the turnstile that I loosened and picked a spot in the left field bleachers which conveniently blocked the view of that entry point unless you were within 30 or 40 feet.

I watched for my opening and usually within 5 minutes I was in and seated in the sunshine. By the 3rd inning I knew which seats would were soon to be mine.

Close to home plate was the place to be where you could hear the ball pop in the catcher's mitt, hear the ump call out ball and strikes, and see the tobacco juice spit all over the dugout. All for free.

There was the smell of cigar smoke and hot dogs and the roar of the happy crowd when we made a great play or even hit a harmless long fly ball.

The constant yelling by the vendors for cold beer and hot dogs, the chit chat and valuable baseball knowledge being passed all around you and of course the traditional "Take me out to the ball game" at the 7th inning stretch.

Nothing better. Warm sun, fun loving people all around, and Halsey Hall himself chomping on a fat stogie and coughing and chocking in the broadcast booth.

I attend the 1965 All Star game and the World Series that year too. Both at Met Stadium Both free and unforgettable.

As a bonus, I was able to get the autographs of some of the all-time great players like Henry Aaron and Harmon Killebrew.

Chapter 4

Minneapolis is a great music city. In the 1960's, we were hoppin and bobbin to Sam and the Storm Troopers or some rock and roll band.

The Beatles performed at Metropolitan Stadium basically on the pitcher's mound. The acoustics were like listening to a 45-record playing on your old record player down in the basement.

That evening, on Saturday August 21, 1965, myself and 25,000 other music lovers, watched and listened to the performance. The ambulances were in use to ferry the fainting girls. The major difference between me and the rest of the audience was they were paying customers and I was once again like during baseball season enjoying the historic performance gratis.

My surreptitious entry this time was by way of scaling a huge I beam which contained a 3-foot patch of grease about 15 feet up.

I was on a greased pole so to speak but going upwards until I reached the chain link fence which I climbed over.

I was in. I even wore the same grease-stained clothes to school the next day as a momento of last night's party.

I had a ball. Ironically, I became an usher at the Met a few years later and was able to see many games for free and get paid for it. I did not care where people sat and was only interested in the game. Didn't even check to see if they had a ticket.

Metropolitan Stadium that historic colossus of Minneapolis was demolished eventually, and the Mall of America sits in its place. The sad ending of an era.

Chapter 5

Like I said, Minneapolis is a great music city. There were dance clubs throughout the city and suburbs where local bands and even a nationally known one would perform.

There was MacGoos on Nicollet Avenue and Lake Street. The Barn out in the country, The Prison, Uncle Sams where the first disco was established in downtown Minneapolis with its lit up plexiglass floor and booming bass speakers.

I would in later years be employed by a local company which outfitted discos all over the country and from that I was to begin the planning of my move north to become a sculptor.

With the freedom of having a car, I was able to see and experience a whole new world. I frequently did that at high speed.

Gas was a quarter a gallon and you could fill your tank for $5.00. There's nothing like the feeling of being pinned to the driver's seat when you push the accelerator to the floor.

The blue smoke of burning rubber when the traffic lights turns green, the screech of the tires on the asphalt, and if there is a passenger along, the wide eyed look in their face and their hand white knuckled gripping the arm rest.

Such was the case when Bruce and I went out to the new Minneapolis Airport which was still under construction in my 1964 Oldsmobile F-85. We tore down the dirt road past large piles of excavated earth Bruce with stopwatch in hand.

We stopped the car when we figured we had travelled at almost 100 miles per hour. Then I decided that we could turn around and race back in the opposite direction. What I didn't realize that there was not enough room to safely stop the car until it was too late.

I rolled from dirt pile to dirt pile in a semi zig zag but the last dirt pile was too high and the car gently rolled to its side ending our journey.

We managed to right the car and made it home without scratch.

I met Bruce in the 3rd grade where we were thrown together with 20 some other little waifs to begin our remedial education.

Bruce was the smartest guy in the class, Good guy with a good sense of humor and his mother was the den mother of our cub scout troop.

His father a, parking lot attendant in downtown Minneapolis, was instrumental in helping us to create an observatory on top of a tree.

Little did he know that most of the material was "borrowed" from a near by construction sight, But he only helped with the planning of our walled hut 15 feet in the air on top of a large elm that he topped for us.

We did all the work and hauled the material atop 2 wagons. After all, it was going to be our own little obeservatory where we could fold open the roof and see the stars with our telescopes. We played mumbly peg an old game in which a jack knife was flipped off from shoulders, wrists, elbows and knees and hopefully stuck point first into the ground. The person who finished sticking the knife first was awarded 3 whacks of the knife handle in to the yop of a sharpened stick in an effort to drive the Stick (or peg) as far into the ground as he could. If you lost, it was your job to pull the peg out of the ground using only your teeth. We always played in Bruce's front yard and scouted the area to make sure of the whereabouts of any dog crap. I think he knew what made me tick. Later, he labeled me a free thinker. like I said, he was smart and perceptive

I got my first job when I was 15 washing dishes at a neighborhood pizza parlor. I was fired 3 weeks later when the manager found out that I was too you by on year.

I was told to come back when I turned 16 and so I did. My future for the next 3 years was set and the good life was now mine for the next 3 years.

I set my sights on buying my first car and with the money I saved I bought a nice 1964 Oldmobile F-85

It was 1965 a historic years for Minneapolis in serveral ways.

The Beatles performed at Metropolitan Stadium for their first and only appearance in Minnesota on August 25th, Ambulances were parked outside just in case they were needed to cart off hysterical and fainting teen aged girls 2l was used to being in the stadium as I had VIP access by way of a crescent wrench It was my pass key.

Liek a cat burglar, I undid the bolts holding the bolts on the bars of the turnstiles. I carefully chose which one to open up so I could squeeze through.

The one beyond the left field fence which was about as far away from curious people who could see what I was up to as you could get.

Chapter 6

The muscle cars of the 1960's was built at the factory for drag racing. You could go into MacGoos, hear the band, maybe dance and eat some pizza. Then it was time to go racing on lake Street. Lake Street was perhaps the preeminent non sanctioned drag strip in Minnesota. The street itself is a regular city street with stop lights every 3 or 4 blocks.

There were a lot of people hitch hiking down the street. I picked up as many as would fit in my Chevy van and someone would usually offer to host a party at their place for everyone that was aboard.

I had a minor part in the music industry in Minneapolis. I started a speaker manufacturing company called Speaker Street located on 48th Street and Grand Avenue.

Myself and 4 others packed our things into a 1965 Chevy station wagon and in the dead of winter headed for Fort Lauderdale Florida looking for work in the construction business.

The gas tank almost fell off in Wisconsin, so we put rope beneath it and tied the 2 ends together after passing it through the rear windows.

We made it through to the 80-degree warmth and sunshine and spent the next 3 months playing football on the beach and snatching oranges and grapefruits from nearby trees. Work had dried up down there. We plotted the start of a stereo speaker manufacture and sales business.

We arrived back in Minnesota in that same worn out 1965 station wagon in the dead of winter still wearing our summer clothes.

On the way, we were running dangerously low on gas somewhere in Alabama late at night. We hailed a police car and Buford the local sheriff informed us that the nearest gas station was about 20 miles up the road. Fearing that we would run out before we could make it, we waited until the man drove off and I pulled into a nearby gas station that was of course closed.

After junior had left and I whispered screw you under my breath, I went exploring and fould an old tar paper shack that was nearm but not on my property. Not wanting to enter it because it belonged to some one else, I decided to wait and find a way to buy the property that it was situated on.

Thanks to my Aunt Barbara who moved on and bequeathed me the $5,00 that the kand with the shack was on I was now able to, after 2 years, get out of the weather and move into a tiny tar paper shack filled with spiders, mice, snakes, and woodland critters.

At last a real roof over me. I don't think I was ever grateful before and to this day happy with such a great feeling of freedom. My diet consisted of raspberry tea, flower tops right off the stalk, occasional bear meat, venison, fish, and my staple, rice and beans with vinegar.

Water was plentiful and readily available in the streams trickling through the sphagnum mosses. I usually purified it by putting in a drop of iodine or boiling it. Giardia is not a very fun thing to get.

Crapper Jr. would be charging me maybe a quarter a crap what with the volume of feces it would force out. Quite the lucrative business in crap. All one needs to become a crap entrepreneur is a brief case, suit, and a willingness to find the crap law violaters wherever they may be.

Chapter 7

There just happened to be an air hose that was shoved through an opening in the station's garage door, so I yanked it hard and a loud rush of air could be heard from the air compressor it was attached to. Fearing the return of that sheriff, it was a harried scramble to use that hose for siphoning gas out of some U-haul trucks that were parked there. It was enough to get us to an open station and we drove on into the night.

In the spring, we decided to take my van to Chicago. No planning, just set sail in the middle of the night. We traveled on into the night and arrived in the big city when it was daylight.

We bought dozens of raw speakers from a wholesale dealer there. We would make the cabinets in the basement and displayed the finished product in the store front upstairs.

The store was christened Speaker Street a take off of the radio program Beaker Street in Little Rock, Arkansas heard on late night FM radio across America, like WLS in Chicago. Although the speaker cabinets were custom expensive hardwoods, and sounded as good as any on the market, we failed within a year.

I moved the operation across the street, but it was a wood working shop now. The tiny space was just large enough for my wood working tools. I slept beneath my table saw.

Since my appliances were limited to a hot plate and there was no shower, refrigerator, or storage, I existed but did not prosper. I bathed in the swimming pool in the park across the street under cover of darkness. Many times, I would turn in pop bottles and cans for the deposit which was 3 cents in order to get a candy bar or two in return.

At thanksgiving, I and another homeless man (technically I wasn't homeless I slept under the roof of my wood shop) ate a good meal at a soup kitchen on the West Bank of the University of Minnesota.

Chapter 8

It was in May of 1972 and the Vietnam war was casting its insidious shadow over the world.

I was caught in a riot that began as an anti-war protest. I found myself running for my life from the Minneapolis and St. Paul police departments who were swinging riot batons and tear gassing everyone with in reach at the University of Minnesota.

Its origin was a result of the United States' air force's bombing of neighboring Cambodia, an escalation of the war most Americans were opposed to.

I was a student there at that time and was taken by complete to see cops charging into the crowd of students many of whom were simply there as I was and now were galloping across the lawn on the mall trying to flee their pursuers.

It was soon after the deadly shootings at Kent State University where 4 students were gunned down by the Ohio National Guard. Four dead in Ohio is a tribute song to that event written by Crosby Stills Nash and Young. Many students were gathered at Coffman Memorial Union Hall that evening watching the televised events of that day's protest turned police riot.

It was announced that the Minnesota National Guard had been summoned. Tensions were heightened over this news. I was a Senior at the U and had ben accepted at the University of San Diego Law School.

A dream come true with lots of money to be had from people who mostly just needed to have their story heard.

That day's events changed my life. I decided that I wasn't going to join.

Chapter 9

I began my adventurous journey with a new and more worthwhile goal as a sculptor.

Five years later, I found myself living in an old canvas military tent in the wilderness of Northern Minnesota near Ely.

After 2 years of living in the rain and cold (it would get cold as 45 below zero) and I had no choice but to grit my chattering teeth and try to keep as warm as I could. I moved into a tar paper shack and that was on the property, but I waited until I bought that property and thanks to my aunt Barbara who I only met once as a child willed me enough money to get it. This shack, filled with spiders, mice, snakes and critters, was a great place though compared to my previous dwelling and I was extremely happy and thankful for it.

The tar paper shack was a roof over my head, and it provided good shelter from the brutal cold. It was often cold in there too until I found a used barrel wood stove. Prior to that, my humble little shack in the Northwoods only had a wood cookstove for heat. Of course, it doubled as a cooking stove too.

I spent the next 7 years remodeling and adding on to it with aspen logs I cut, hauled, and peeled then carefully fit together. It would make me one complete day to make a round, that is to fit together one layer all around the building.

My haven burnt to the ground during a blue moon on New Year's Eve, 1990.

This was the land of lakes and woods. Home of the Ojibwe tribe, our hosts, where only a few people lived scattered and sparse it is solitude and a place of reverence away from the belching smoke and noise of the concrete city.

Instead, here is ancient granite and healthy clean air, green trees, found in Northern climates like white pines, red pines, black spruce, birch, tamarck, cedar, balsam and many aspen.

Many clean lakes and rivers, few roads, and cars and everything a person needs to live a simple and great life. It is inspiring and now my new home in the land of the free trapper.

I pitched my canvas tent on a little knoll amongst the balsam and birch trees a flat place with rocks and boulders scattered amongst the grass and broad leaf astor.

Nearby was a concrete basement without a roof that was once used as a payhouse for the Mud Creek back in the early 1900's. I built a makeshift bed of balsam boughs that I chopped off from dead birch trees and bound them together into a crude but effective bed frame I topped it with balsam boughs and set my wool blankets and grandma's fur coat on top of my green needled mattress.

I arranged rocks that I found nearby in a circle and topped my new firepit with an old refrigerator grate found in the dump and then pitched my tent.

Chapter 10

It was minus 40 and I sat in the fire truck with Chief Klun of the Ely Fire department and watched as it burned to the ground.

I lost everything I owned.

It was minus 40 and I sat in that fire truck with only a T-shirt on as I was extremely hot and panicked from trying to put out the fire.

I raced to my neighbor's house, Buster Nicholson, which was 7 miles away with 3 feet of snow on the ground and burst through his back door yelling, "MY HOUSE IS ON FIRE!"

"USE THE PHONE!" he hollered.

The Ely Fire Department dropped their New Year's Eve celebration and met me at the beginning of Mud Creek Road and I hoped in the truck with Chief Klun and we led the fire trucks to my haven 6 miles into the woods.

Too late.

Fire had engulfed my home.

Glass and ammunition were exploding.

Hoses on the fire truck were frozen.

A night to remember.

I knocked on my old friend's door, Phil (Peppy) Potterjoy, and when Peppy answered the door, around midnight, he said:

"Happy New Year!"

And I replied, "not really" and explained what had happened.

I spent the next 2 weeks on his couch. But if anything was going to motivate me after losing all I had, and homeless in the winter in the woods, it was this.

31 years later, I created the monumental sculpture of a resolute and powerful Viking which is now the second largest cement human figure in Minnesota.

It was a yearlong endeavor.

He stands with his sword rammed into the ground looking sky ward for a sign from the heavens.

Just as I did in 1973 and on New Year's Eve.

Chapter 11

The man that came walking into my camp was dressed in a suit and wore glasses.

He had a small brief case and I surmised that he looked like a government agent. He walked up and introduced himself as a county inspector. What could he possibly want?

Here I was living in a tent and I had no idea how he knew that I was even here.

The question from him was "where are you going to the toilet?" I didn't think anyone would care as I was far off the beaten path, but I guess not far enough, so I told him,

"See that log that you just stepped over, about 2 feet off the ground? It makes a perfect seat for crapping and reading."

He then told me that, with a dead serious look, that what I was doing wasn't allowed and then he showed me some papers, one of which was an application for an outhouse permit, and the other was a plan for building an outhouse which looked like a blue print for building a small fort with a cement basement.

My idea was simpler and cost nothing. His idea was much more elaborate and pretty costly. Besides, why put up more buildings when a log will do? The animals that are out here all use the simplest means to an end, that being just taking a crap and they are on their way. But it was now going to cost me a dime every time I took a crap.

Chapter 12

After junior had left and I whispered screw you under my breath, I went exploring and found an old tar paper shack that was near, but not on my property.

Not wanting to enter it because it belonged to someone else, I decided to wait and find a way to buy the property that it was situated on.

Thanks to my Aunt Barbara who moved on and bequeathed me the $5,000 that the land with the shack was on I was now able to, after 2 years, get out of the weather and move into a tiny tar paper shack filled with spiders, mice, snakes, and woodland critters.

At last, a real roof over me. I don' t think I was ever that grateful before and to this day happy with such a great feeling of freedom. My diet consisted of raspberry tea, flower tops right off the stalk, occasional bear meat, venison, fish, and my staple, rice and beans with vinegar.

Water was plentiful and readily available in the streams trickling through the sphagnum mosses. I usually purified it by putting in a drop of iodine or boiling it. Giardia is not a very fun thing to get.

Crapper Jr. would be charging me maybe a quarter a crap what with the volume of feces it would force out.

Quite the lucrative business in crap. All one needs to become a crap entrepreneur is a brief case, suit, and a willingness to find the crap law violators wherever they may be.

Chapter 13

———✑———

The days were spent exploring and hunting.

My diet consisted mainly of venison and rabbit with coffee made over my campfire.

Rabbits were snared with a flexible wire loop and fitted with a swivel and lock so as to tightened under pressure.

Rabbits were plentiful and relatively easy to find as they travelled up and down deer trails instead of fighting their way through the brush.

Deer are plentiful but much harder to bag as they are much more wary. I thought this is the way to live, just a rifle and some snares out in the woods and matching wits with the wildlife in the woods getting my food.

My nights, wrapped in my fur coat and wool blankets, were a fantastic journey through dream land as my dreams were very vivid. The flying dream, where I could simply jump in the air and like some wingless bird were very common and I could go as far and high as I wanted.

I dreamt of a rabbit in one of my snares and the next morning after a deep and relaxing sleep, I trudged my way up and down the hazel and dogwood filled hills and just like in my dream I found a rabbit in one of my snares.

Although an idyllic life, when the rains and thunder came crashing down on me inside my canvas tent, being cooped up inside my tent for a week or however long the rains fell, could be a depressing way to spend time, like listening to someone constantly complaining not unlike rain dripping from the eaves.

I lived in a hole in the ground actually it was an old minning building concrete basement from mining days I built a roof over it from tamarck trees I cut in a nearby swamp and took them out on a cable with another cable with another cable attached with a pulley Sort of like ancient Indians who sometimes lived in a hole in the ground. The log repurposed later into the walls of the cabin that burned.

Here they come trudging through the woods in their suits and dresses with shiny shoes carrying some sort of pamphlet entitled AWAKE Apparently these people were like a flock of rooosters who found me out here to get out of bed and get busy before I was barbequed Jumping Jehova It was the Witnesses come to save me!

Chapter 14

My new home was made of small cedar logs stacked vertically and sealed with rolled or as the old timers used to call it mule hide roofing nailed to the logs to help keep out the draft and any critters that may seek shelter there.

It measured about 10 feet wide by 12 feet long and had an old wooden floor covered in linoleum.

It had a sleeping loft with room enough for my fur coat and wool blankets.

It had a peaked roof which was weather tight and a couple of small windows that let in light and would open to get some ventilation in the little but in the clearing atop a hill that the shack was located on.

It had a wood cook stove that not only provided some heat but also afforded me the luxury of cooking indoors out of the weather. It took some experience to learn how to use the stove for cooking so that the food was not over done but cooked enough so that it was edible.

My attempts to bake bread proved fruitless and I used the failed concoction for minnow bait that I trapped in the beaver pond down the hill from the shack.

I bartered the bait at the local resort down at the end some 5 miles away at the end of Mud Creek Road.

What I received for the bait in exchange was beer and company at the bar where I would go to seek some human companionship.

Chapter 15

It was now 1984 and my new home needed a remodel so that I could have more living space.

I had an old Homelght chainsaw and I began to cut down the popple or aspen trees in order to remake the old mule hide shack which served as a horse barn in earlier days.

I had about 3 or 4 hundred dollars left over from the purchase of my new piece of land with that old horse barn turned cool log cabin in the woods.

It was not going to last me forever and minnow trapping for barter was not going to get me very far.

It was time to get serious and get a job so that I could remodel my living quarters in a better and more pleasing to the eye fashion. I got a job at Bear Head Lake State Park as a foreman of a brushing crew that brushed out the trails in the State Park.

It was the same 4 guys that showed up every morning at 8 A.M. in order to grab the chain saw and some brush hooks and head out in the woods to make the trails that the tourists would use when we finished them.

They were only supposed to work for 2 weeks and then they were to be replaced by others who were standing in line for a job. There were no others in line.

I went to the employment office and told them that although there should be next one who registered with the government for emergency employment that there were in fact no prospects to brush trails in Bear Head Lake State Park.

I asked and received permission to keep these 4 working as long as the funding lasted.

If you wanted and needed a job you could have one.

Chapter 16

We built trail shelters from logs we logged in the park. It was spruce and as long as we had to remove them from the trails we might as well use them for building our shelters where the tourists could take a break from hiking Arbuckle, as we nick named him because he was overweight, managed to almost get a case of hypothermia while out brushing and there was no one to meet as promised at the time and place decided upon. I ran to the shop some 3 miles away, and proceeded to curse out the man who didn't show up but was instead drinking coffee and whooping up in the garage.

I' d like to think that my anger led to a job in the future with the Minnesota DNR.

It was customary back in those days to hire a logger and a portable saw mill to saw the trees into building materials.

After having secured my regular full-time job at Bear Head Lake State Park, I hired Bruce Kainz as the logger and Roger Porrisch as the logger to saw not only the red and white pines for my soon to be new home in the woods.

But first we needed to flatten two sides of the aspen logs that I had pealed and limbed ready for log building. I had the 50 to 60 logs flattened on two sides so that all I had to do was saddle notch the ends accurately and the cabin would be quickly, as quickly as reasonable, be remodeled.

Chapter 17

I met Peppy, also known as Kimbo the Clown, from his tap dance days. He is a gentle giant of a man who stands about 6 1/2 feet tall and weighs about 300 pounds.

He was working at Merl Thorns Union 76 gas station in Ely and was changing a flat tire on my '67 Ford pickup truck.

Peppy had graduated from Ely Memorial High School back in 1970. He owned land, with his wife Cathy, he bought from Merl on Robinson Lake and is married to Cathy, also known as Mary, who came from New Mexico, and graduated from Silver Bay High School in 1973. Cathy is one of the greatest cooks ever to live in the Great North Woods.

They bought the land and there after moved to New Mexico in search of work as the iron ore mines of Northern Minnesota were pretty much shut down at that time.

Peppy and Cathy returned to their beloved trailer on Robinson Lake about a year later and found that Merl had tried to horn swaggle on their deal for their land.

The Thorns were from California and although here before I arrived in the North Woods, did not have a real good reputation.

Peppy handled Merl in his usual calm, cool, and collected way and Merl did not last much longer as Ely entrepreneur.

"Yippee O aye Kayi I' m an old cowboy from the Rio Grande----"

I can just hear Pep singing this song in his living room with the brightly colored fish darting around in his lit up aquarium.

Chapter 18

The wolves finally got of Lem my only friend and best companion. I could have killed many of them by snaring rabbits and putting some anti-freeze near the dead bait rabbit but I didn't as that would have done nothing to get my old partner back.

He got out somehow while I was at work and like before he was determined to be with me and they were laying in wait for him. It was like the time that he flipped his dog house on its roof while chained to it to follow me to work.

I buried Lemmon out in the woods where I found is body. It was as if they knew that he would be alone eventually and they were biding their time when they could safely attack.

They knew somehow that this was the time. I have and still have had many dreams of wolves lurking in the bush just waiting and being patient for something to attack and kill for food.

This was my only partner and true friend in life, Lemmon my best friend and partner, who I went through many adventures out in the woods together with.

It is the way things go something dies in order that other life may live on. This was the legacy of Lemmon the tough, blind dog who died so that the wolves could have a meal that they may live on. It was going to be a new life without him but I would carry on and do what I had to do.

Chapter 19

Through the Eyes of a Wolf

The burning rose colored dawn in realms of azure blue and yellow fingered skies, melts in the golden gleam of her wilderness cool pool eyes.

Ebony raw claws arcing towards the flashing glory like black granite jutting from an ancient lake bed to pulsing grey skies. Biting breezes ripple the tawny flecked fur as an almighty voice from a great-heart-glories in her great ears. Cedars in the emerald mist with flashes of silver smoke stream through the sweet-smelling morning air to her wet nose.

The yellow bejeweled wild eyes see the wilderness magic. I see them gathered out in the woods outside waiting, watching, silent shadowy four-legged meat eaters roaming and listening for a chance to kill and eat. Watchful eyes see through the brush and leaves your very presence felt within her entire being.

She is silent and waiting. As the colors pulsate across the night sky, shimmering clouds of skylight glow bright green and yellow tinged with blue and silver stretching from horizon to horizon. She loosens her in a mournful howl into the night air. Her breath comes with the wild voice from the deepest part of her lungs.

I feel like I can make a connection with her, a soulful connection but she doesn't want much to do with me. There must be something we have in common. Two souls on the perimeter of life' s shores, but she is wild and free to live her life while I am a prisoner of my limited point of view.

The ghostly night light with her purple legions soon covered the sky. The moon began to rise in the sky and in the mystical glowing light her haunting howl rose deep within her proud chest.

Do you believe in what God has in store for you?

Why not?

Do you believe in what God has in store for the wolf?

Why not?

Because we do not know the answer. Maybe the wolf does. Do you believe in living a dream? I bet the wolf does. The Great Creator of the Universe has given us the gift of this earth. We are guests here in our travels.

Chapter 20

I told Lemmon when I buried him that I would continue on and I did.

With Peppy's help, I was able to put in a large plate glass window that was slanted at a 45-degree angle for solar heating.

I had one important thing in common with Lemmon. His blindness and my new surroundings.

Both of us had to adapt to what was next.

Lemmon was done adapting and I carried on without him.

We had both been cold in the horse barn but I was determined to make things cozier.

I scooped up gravel and rock from the road and placed it underneath the floor of the new solar room to make a heat sink for the warmth of the sun.

I made a rock wall that I put behind the wood stove that would absorb heat from the fire at night and would radiate heat back during the day.

I tried getting Lemmon to sleep with me but he refused and slept on the cabin floor.

The rock wall with an archway built in the middle of it had a small door in it that I could close to keep in as much heat as I could instead of going out through the large plate glass window at night.

The cabin got a little more cozy and warm as time went by but it was a lonely life as there was no one to share life with.

I was able to add on and get more living room by putting up logs that I had cut, peeled, and put together.

It was so hot that it melted a horseshoe that was in the burned cabin.

Chapter 21

Like being on a giant roulette wheel, my number came up again and this time it cost me everything that I owned. I was out hunting deer one afternoon and I hadn't seen any food in the woods so I started back to the cabin around sun down.

I stepped in a hole in the ground and twisted my knee, an injury that still hurts to this day. I spent the night out in the woods crawling on my hands and knees, getting poked in the eyes with brush, and falling a few feet off from a cliff.

I was hallucinating, seeing cabins with lights that weren't there. I was dehydrated craving of all things, cherry juice. I managed to get back just in time to see the sun come up and I drank cup after cup of water.

It was not very cold for November, and I was not cold, I was instead hot and sweating from having fought my way through the brush all night. I promised God that I would never forget and I haven't.

He helped me get through the night. The day that I decided to swim across Buckshot Lake was probably over 90 degrees. The lake was small and I used it for snagging pike with a treble hook baited with leeches that I had trapped.

It was an illegal set line posted from tree to tree across a south bay in the lake. It was one of the happiest days when I could bush whack back home with a pike large enough to feed me on a stringer. I decided that not only would I swim across the lake, but that I would swim back across it to get my clothes and shoes. About half way back, I couldn't make it. I knew I was going to drown and no one would ever know what happened to me.

Then I put my feet down, resigned to death in a meaningless way, and found I was 4 feet of water.

Chapter 22

When Spring arrived with it's warming sun, the snow that had made it's way into my underground concrete home turned it into a swimming pool, so I was forced to move outdoors with no shelter. I cut the tamarack roof poles into firewood for future warming campfires.

I then began to make a new campsite using some of the poles and balsam boughs to enclose my new living quarters. (70) (237)

It was only temporary as I needed more of a building for the upcoming winter and to shelter me and my belongings from the rains.

The horse barn that I had remodeled into a cozy cabin after 7 years of laborious years with aspen logs that I cut, hauled, peeled, and carefully fit together, burned to the ground during a blue moon on New Year's Eve 1990.

It was minus 40 and I was homeless out in the woods. Again. I fought against the fire having no water and wearing only a T-shirt because of the intense heat. I made a disastrous mistake which led to the complete destruction of my home in the woods. I had essentially put out the fire which engulfed the ceiling by shoveling snow onto the cabin floor and throwing it up and onto the blazing ceiling. The fire was extinguished.

I was exhausted and very hot. I climbed up on the roof and cut a hole in it in order to shovel snow down upon the glowing roof rafters. As soon as I finished cutting the hole, the entire roof exploded in flames and I knew that all was lost. I raced to the neighbor's house, Buster Nicholson, who lived 7 miles away, with 3 feet of snow in the woods.

I had been visiting relatives during the holidays and came home New Year's Eve to a cabin that was 40 below zero. I usually lit the cabin with kerosene lights and candles so I was used to the glow that came from this lighting.

But the light that night was much brighter than normal, and that is because the ceiling was on fire. I burst through Buster' s back door without knocking, screaming that my house was on fire and he yelled at me to use the phone to call the Ely Fire Department.

Chapter 23

As I sat in the fire truck with Chief Klun, I realized that I had lost everything that I owned except the clothes that I was wearing, the pickup truck that I was driving and the chain saw I used to cut a hole in the ill-fated cabin roof.

What had taken me 7 years to build was now gone along with everything that I had owned in about 7 hours. I asked Chief Klun if the fire department could let the cabin completely burn to the ground to save on the cleanup and he said they could as long as I did not have insurance and I didn't so they let it burn.

The hoses were frozen so they had no water to put the fire out anyway so next was finding a place to spend the night' He told me that I could spend the night in the Ely jail so as to have a roof over my head but I declined his offer and instead went to Peppy' s house and knocked on the door around midnight. He answered with a hearty happy New Year and the expression on my face must have told him that I was not in a celebrating mood.

I didn't quite know what to say so I blurted out that my cabin had just burned down and that I would need a place to stay for a night or two.

He welcomed me in and said that I was welcome to the couch.

Chapter 24

I spent the next several weeks camped out on Peppy's couch trying to put together a plan to move onwards.

I remembered much of life and how it was living in my little cabin. I remember the bear that I shot and cooked on the old wood cook stove, canning venison, and the cabin itself with its warm wood stove and its small but functioning kitchen.

The moose that would occasionally clip clop its way up to the cabin, the weasels that I would hand feed trapped mice to, the rabbits I would snare and rely on for food. The minnow trapping that I would barter for beer at the Glenwood Lodge.

There was no shortage of memories of this simple life. A giant tree crashes in the mystical moonlit night on the full moon of Halloween.

I could not live on memories, I needed to proceed and start over with a new cabin in the woods.

I bought a pickup camper for $300 and settled in for the rest of winter.

My work was about to begin anew.

Everything that you would want in a decade of a woods adventure except the losing of everything I owned and having to start over in the cold was but a memory.

It was the beginning of realizing my dream of being a sculptor out in the woods.

Learn to forget.

I was 40 years old and about to begin on my biggest projects of my life and they would take me to new heights of adventure and accomplishment.

EPILOGUE

I built a house with 7 gables like the novelist Nathaniel Hawthorne. For the first time in 42 years, I have a warm house. Sitting atop a rickety old over loaded tourist bus, hurtling down a Steep, winding road with sheer cliffs and a 500 foot drop off on one side like some Bolivian death road, with a tequila gulping driver who can' t see the brake pedal, we are balancing on 2 wheels Careening around the dangerous corners with disaster just a few feet Away. Will there be a sign of living or is the Music Over? * The Doors "It' s a long, long journey so stay by my side. When I walk through the storm You'll be my guide" ** The Seekers 1964.

"So, let's have a drink together before leaving our temporary homes and meet again in heaven --- the only place better than the woods."

Largest Cement Human Figure in Minnesota

At 9:19 P.M. I entered this life and opened my wary eyes. I am the youngest son of Ken Petersen (1926-1977) and Bernice Rohne (1929-2020). Largely anonymous childhood with only minor police troubles. Good at reading and writing from an early age thanks to my mother who encouraged me and my ambitious ways. I went on to attend the University of Minnesota from 1970 to 1973. I am known as a friend to strangers.

Postscript

Since writing Sculptor of the North, I have become a one handed sculptor and fallen on hard times. Stay tuned for the sequel featuring my works. Don't ever give up.